This book is dedicated to my brother Bobby

All images, photos and text copyright © 2011 by Katherine M. Migaki.

Alphabet Denver first published in the United States in 2011 by I See It Press.

ISBN 13: 978-0-9834-6200-2

Library of Congress Catalogue information on request.
1.   English language-Alphabet-Juvenile literature.

Cover and interior design by Kerrie Lian, under contract with MacGraphics Services: www.MacGraphics.net

Printed in Canada by Friesens

I See It Press
Email: Kitty@AlphabetDenver.com
Website: www.AlphabetDenver.com

A GPS ALPHABET HUNT BOOK

ALPHABET

DENVER

KITTY MIGAKI

I SEE IT
PRESS

ALPHABET

ROUND TOWN

ONGITUDE AND LATITUDE

OEMS TO READ

ARD TO FIND

CROBAT LETTERS

UILD BRAIN CONNECTIONS

DUCATIONAL

AKE YOUR PHOTO

**D** ISCOVER

**E** VERYWHERE YOU LOOK

N EW WAYS TO SEE

V ERY FUN

E VERYONE CAN PLAY

**R** HYMES TO LEARN

A

39°44.224'
-104°59.368'

A is always first.

Up-side

Down-side

Left-side

Right-side

A is always first.

HINT: the compass colors are the same for those letters close together.

A

39°744.253'
-104°986.124'

B is bright.
He lights up the night.
If you come by day,
B won't look this way.

A **B**

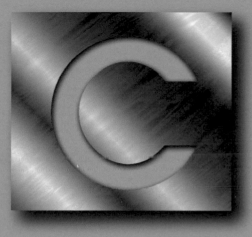

39°44.738'
-104°59.917'

Do you see the C?
C can see you,
you see.
She is in disguise,
you see.
She hides inside the C,
you see.

A B C

D

39°44.627′
-104°59.276′

There once was a letter named D.
Who thought he was special like B.
But D didn't know
That B had a glow
That you too can go and see.

A B C D

Skinny Superstructure E
extra strong is she
look around find more than one

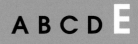

F

39°44.220'
-104°59.357'

*You have to stand
in the right spot,
or an F
it is not!*

A B C D E **F**

39°43.574'
-104°59.203'

G AND HIS FRIENDS ARE ON THE FENCE.

WHEN NO ONE'S AROUND,

THEY TRY TO GET DOWN.

NONE OF THEM HAS MUCH SENSE.

A B C D E F **G**

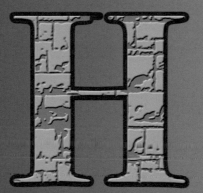

39°45.723'
-104°56.415'

Don't look small,

look tall.

Don't look skinny,

look fat.

Don't look dark,

look light.

How many H's do you see?

I see two,

How about you?

A B C D E F G **H**

I

39°43.574'
-104°59.203'

I know a letter named I

Who watches as bikes roll by

She lives on a creek

Where she can peek

At bikers and joggers all week

A B C D E F G H **I**

J

39°44.726′
-105°0.635′

Jumpin' Jive J!

June, July, J!

Jennifer, Jeffery, Jessica, J!

Jazzy, Jiffy, Jelly, J!

Hey, hey, hey!

Try hard as you may,

It's tough to find a J.

A B C D E F G H I J

K

39°45.221'
-105°0.630'

There once was a letter named K.

Who was exceedingly gray.

She hangs around,

Upside down,

On the bridge where she stays all day.

ABCDEFGHIJ K

39°45.051'
-104°59.533'

L

Looking Lucky L

Looking Lovely L

Looking Lively L

Looking Swell L

Can you tell, where is the L?

A B C D E F G H I J K **L**

m & m & m & m.

can you see lots of them?

A B C D E F G H I J K L M

N

39°44.220'
-104°59.357'

You can see right through the N.

Have you been inside with him?

If your answer is no,

I encourage you to go.

The Art is part

of a great start.

So enjoy it your whole life through,

A gift from others to you.

A B C D E F G H I J K L M N

39°43.574'
-104°59.203'

UH O!
Oh no!
Here we go to find the O.
Not one O,
But rows of O's!
Take a phot-O
Of you, standing in the O!

A B C D E F G H I J K L M N O

P

39°44.669'
-104°59.744'

The P
Near the light rail
Stands alone and keeps watch
Over the hustle and bustle
All day

A B C D E F G H I J K L M N O **P**

39°44.778'
-104°59.585'

OH LETTER Q,
WHAT CAN YOU DO?
YOU MAY BE FIRST IN QUEEN,
BUT FOR THOSE WHO PASS BY,
YOU'RE UNSEEN.

A B C D E F G H I J K L M N O P Q

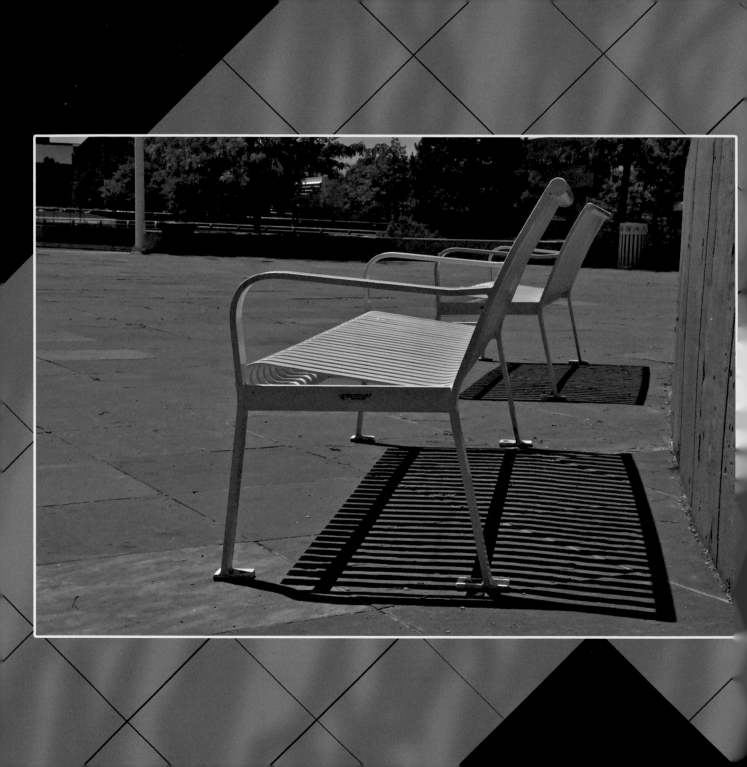

R

39°44.657′
-104°59.964′

There once was an R on the bench.
A girl asked if he could speak French.
He could you know
And just to show
He asked for some fries in French!

A B C D E F G H I J K L M N O P Q R

Super S

Slithers

Slinks and

Slides up

the building

Side

by the

Art Museum.

See him?

39°44.201'
-104°59.334'

A B C D E F G H I J K L M N O P Q R **S**

T

39°45.130'
-105°0.733'

You can take a bike to get there,

you can take a hike to get there.

Either way,

stay all day.

It's not far,

go by car.

If you wish,

stay

and feed the fish!

A B C D E F G H I J K L M N O P Q R S T

39°44.920′
-105°0.996′

Up on the left   Up on the right

Up on the left   Up on the right

Up on the left   Up on the right

Whew!

I think my stomach is upside down!!

A B C D E F G H I J K L M N O P Q R S T **U**

39°44.200′
-104°59.332′

I think I shall never see,
A letter lovely as a V.

A V whose arms give an embrace,
to share a kiss or hug a face.

A V who sees blue sky all day,
And lifts her concrete arms to play.

A V who may in summer rest,
On a mat of grass to look her best.

A V who always plays a part
Is helping us enjoy the art.

A B C D E F G H I J K L M N O P Q R S T U V

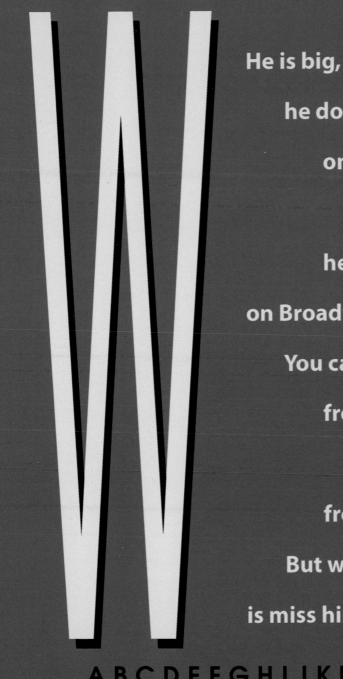

He is big,

he does a jig,

on Broadway.

He is all yellow,

he is a fine fellow,

on Broadway.

You can see him

from your car.

You can see him

from afar.

But what you can't do,

is miss him!

39°42.322'
-104°59.425'

A B C D E F G H I J K L M N O P Q R S T U V **W**

39°45.308′
-104°59.579′

Sung to the tune of "Take Me Out to the Ballgame"

Take me out to the Rockies.
Take me out to the park.
Teach me my letters, find X, Y and Z.
I can see them! Take a photo of me!
´Cause it's search, search, search for the letters,
I must find them by night,
´Cause it's A! B! c d e f when you play the game.

A B C D E F G H I J K L M N O P Q R S T U V W **X**

Y

39°44.956'
-104°57.195'

There was a letter named Y.

Who stood all day as cars passed by.

She lived at the zoo,

But she never knew,

The animals who lived inside!

A B C D E F G H I J K L M N O P Q R S T U V W X **Y**

39°44.563'
-105°1.249'

Look for Z near E.

Z is Mr. Zzzzip.

He may try to give you the slip.

I hope we had fun!

When you find Z,

You're done!

A B C D E F G H I J K L M N O P Q R S T U V W X Y **Z**

Keep track of the letters you find! Place your *Alphabet Denver* stickers here.*

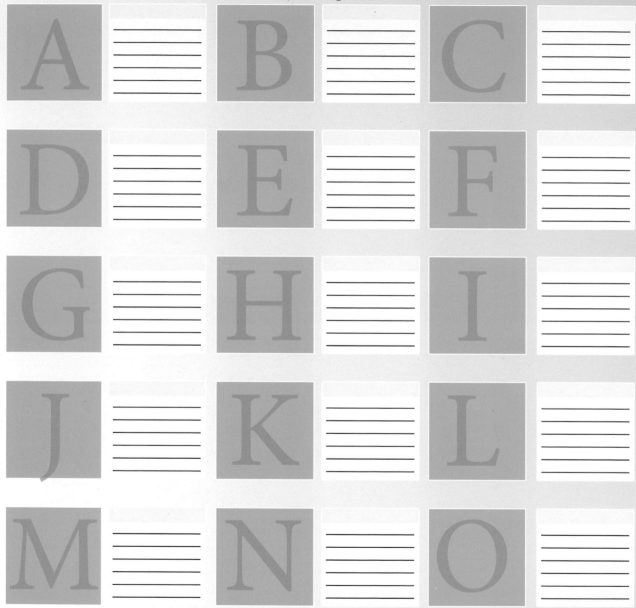

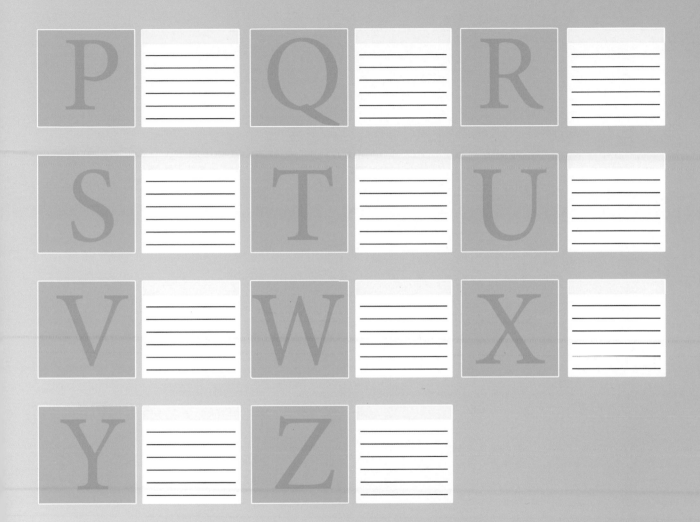

*Stickers available at www.AlphabetDenver.com

Discover 10 Different Types of Poems in *Alphabet Denver*

Type of poem	*Location*	*Description*
Acrostic	Title page	Each letter of an existing word is used to build a new word that describes the original word.
Alliteration	J, L, O, S	The same letter-sound repeats consistently throughout a poem.
Clerihew	Q	Usually about a famous person, this four-line poem consists of two rhymed couplets making the rhyme AABB. Clerihews often poke fun at the subject.
Cinquain	P	A non-rhyming poem with a specific number of syllables per line. The first line is two syllables, second line four syllables, third line six syllables, fourth line eight syllables, and the fifth line is again, two syllables.
Concrete	L, S, T, U, W	A concrete poem is visually presented in the shape of the object about which the poem is written. For example, a concrete poem about a tree would be shaped like a tree.
Haiku	E	This style of poetry, developed in Japan hundreds of years ago, is written with a total of 17 syllables over three lines in a five-syllable, seven-syllable, five-syllable pattern. Traditional haiku does not rhyme, and the subject is nature.
Limerick	D, G, I, K, R, Y	Usually a funny poem of five lines. The first, second, and fifth lines are longest and rhyme with each other. The third and fourth lines are shorter and rhyme together.
Rhyme	A, B, C, F, H, I, M, N, O, Z	In a rhyme, the sound of the word or syllable at the end of one line rhymes with the end of another line. All lines can rhyme, or an end pattern may exist ABAB or AABB.
Song	X	A song is a poem or phrase set to music and intended to be sung.
Sonnet	V	A sonnet typically presents a 14 line poem that uses any number of formal rhyme schemes.

Note: The "V" poem is a tribute to the wonderful poem "Trees" by Alfred Joyce Kilmer.

Suggestions for More Fun

Families:

Grab a camera, your *Alphabet Denver* book, and make a fun outing finding the letters in everyone's name. Or host a letter-hunt birthday party!

Teachers/Home-School Parents:

Use *Alphabet Denver* to teach poetry, photography, map-reading skills, and GPS technology. Most letters are located near field trip destinations. Or, challenge students to find and photograph letters at home and in their neighborhood!

Visitors:

Find the letters at major attractions in downtown Denver! Your group can look for letters hiding at the zoo, museums, stadiums, and more.

Share your photos:

Upload your letter photographs on the *Alphabet Denver* website.

Purchase photographs and stickers:

Decorate kids' rooms with their names or fun words! Frame letter photos to hang at home or office. Stickers for the sticker pages and photographs from the *Alphabet Denver* book can be purchased at:

www.AlphabetDenver.com.

If you have enjoyed looking for letters using your GPS, you may enjoy geocaching.

What is Geocaching?

Players playing the sport of geocaching use a handheld GPS (or smartphone with GPS) to hunt for hidden treasure by locating specific map coordinates. Upon reaching the indicated coordinates, you look for a treasure box and swap a small treasure — a gold dollar, whistle, or small toy, for example — with an item in the box. If there is a log book you can sign it. Track your finds and learn more about geocaching at www.Geocaching.com

You may be surprised to learn that there are more than 1 million people geocaching around the world. According to the website above, downtown Denver has more than 7,000 hidden caches. So get out there, have fun, and learn something new!

Resources used in this book

The author used an Apple iPhone® and the following apps from Apple iTunes®:

1. "Location" app to gather the GPS coordinates.
2. "Redlaser" app to generate and read QR codes.

About the Author and Photographer

There once was a lady named Kitty,
Who thought she was exceedingly witty.
She was only so-so,
Yet her talent would grow,
And now she's a very witty Kitty!

Kitty Migaki lives near Denver, Colorado, where she keeps up with her two kids, her husband, the fish, lizard, dog, chickens, and alpacas – when she isn't squeezing in time to take photographs.

You can write to her or post your own alphabet photos at Kitty@AlphabetDenver.com

About the Designer

Switching careers to graphic design in 1984 allowed Kerrie Lian to realize her long-standing dream of becoming an artist. In 1991 both her daughter, Madison, and her company, Madison Ave. Design, were born. Kerrie lives in Highlands Ranch, Colorado, with her husband Fred, Madison, and their overly affectionate Old English sheepdog Strider.

Letter addresses that are within walking distance of each other are the same color.

A 1310 Bannock St.
Denver, CO 80204

B 1700 Lincoln
Denver, CO 80204

C 1101 13th St.
Denver, CO 80204

D 1700 Broadway
Denver, CO 80204

E 1701 Bryant St.
Denver, CO 80204

F 100 West 14th Ave.
Denver, CO 80204

G Speer and Lincoln
Denver, CO 80204

H Colorado Blvd. &
Martin Luther
King Blvd.
Denver, CO 80205

I Speer and Lincoln
Denver, CO 80204

J 7th St. & Chopper
Blvd.
Denver, CO 80204

K Speer Bridge over I-25

P Corner of 14th & Stout
Denver, CO 80204

L Tabor Center
16th St Mall

Q 16th Street Mall
Denver, CO 80204

M 1531 Champa St.
Denver, CO 80204

R Denver Center for
Performing Arts
Complex

N Denver Art Museum
100 West 14th Ave.
Denver, CO 80204

S 100 West 14th Ave.
Denver, CO 80204

O Speer and Lincoln
Denver, CO 80204

T 700 Water St.
Denver, CO 80211

U 2121 Children's
Museum Dr.
Denver, CO 80211

X 2001 Blake St.
Denver, CO 80205

V 100 West 14th Ave.
Denver, CO 80204

Y 2300 Steele St.
Denver, CO 80204

W 595 South Broadway
Denver, CO 80209

Z 1701 Bryant St.
Denver, CO 80204

If you have difficulty with the longitude
and latitude in the book try the coordinates
below. All letters are in the city of Denver.

A	39.7370	-104.9898	N	39.7377	-104.9895
B	39.7434	-104.9861	O	39.7272	-104.9870
C	39.7446	-104.9980	P	39.7439	-104.9956
D	39.7427	-104.9873	Q	39.7474	-104.9949
E	39.7439	-105.0213	R	39.7439	-104.9991
F	39.7377	-104.9889	S	39.7377	-104.9895
G	39.7266	-104.9871	T	39.7502	-105.0150
H	39.7625	-104.9436	U	39.7515	-105.0150
I	39.7266	-104.9868	V	39.7377	-104.9895
J	39.7474	-104.9949	W	39.7063	-104.9905
K	39.7537	-105.0098	X	39.7552	-104.9931
L	39.7504	-104.9943	Y	39.7510	-104.9507
M	39.7459	-104.9948	Z	39.7439	-105.0213

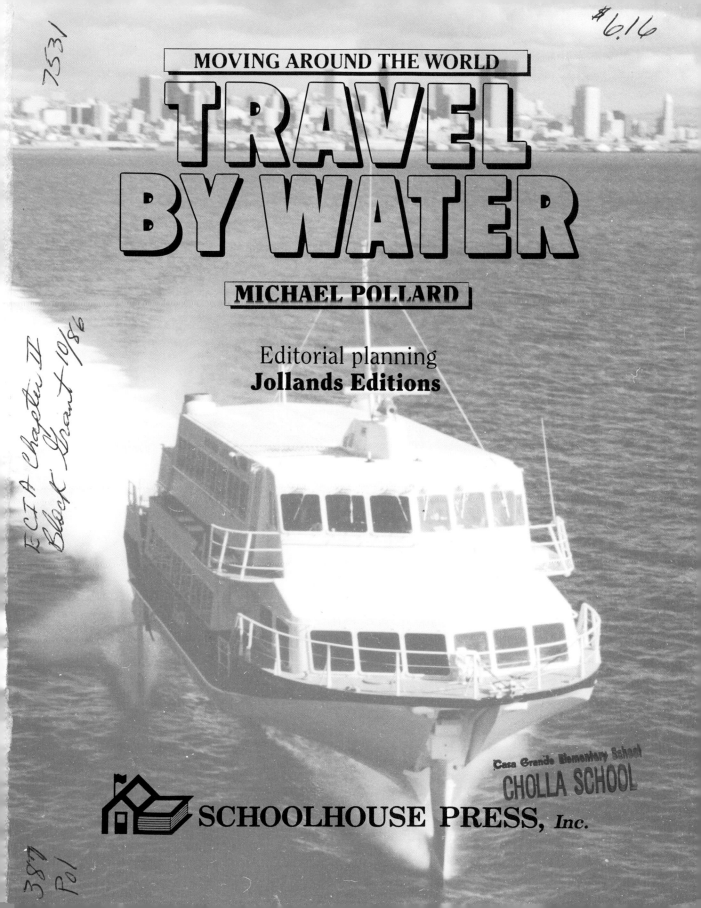

MOVING AROUND THE WORLD

TRAVEL BY WATER

MICHAEL POLLARD

Editorial planning
Jollands Editions

SCHOOLHOUSE PRESS, Inc.

Designed and produced by BLA Publishing Limited,
Swan Court, East Grinstead, Sussex, England.

Also in LONDON · HONG KONG · TAIPEI · SINGAPORE · NEW YORK

A Ling Kee Company

Illustrations by Keith Duran/Linden Artists,
 George Fryer/Linden Artists and BLA Publishing Limited
Colour origination by Clan Studios Limited
Printed in Italy by G. Canale & C. S.p.A. — Torino

85/86/87/88   6 5 4 3 2 1

Acknowledgements
**The Publishers wish to thank the following
organizations for their invaluable assistance in the
preparation of this book.**

Boeing Company
British Caledonian
British Hovercraft Corporation
British Petroleum
Norwegian Caribbean Lines
Racal-Decca Company
Royal National Lifeboat Institution
University of Liverpool

Photographic credits
t = top b = bottom l = left r = right

cover: Boeing Company

4*b* ZEFA; 5*b* Yachting World; 7*b* Philip Sauvain; 19
"Trustees of the Science Museum" (London); 21*t* The
Mansell Collection; 21*b* National Maritime Museum
London; 23*t* The Mansell Collection; 23*b* National
Maritime Museum London; 24*t* ZEFA; 24*b* Mystic
Seaport Museum; 27 ZEFA; 29*t*, 32 University of
Liverpool; 33*t* British Caledonian; 33*b* Norwegian
Caribbean Lines; 34*t*, 34*b*, 35, 38, 39*t* ZEFA; 40 British
Petroleum; 41 ZEFA; 42 Racal-Decca Company; 43*t*
ZEFA; 43*b* Royal National Lifeboat Institution; 44
Boeing Company; 45*t* British Hovercraft Corporation

Note to the reader
In this book there are some words in the text which are printed in **bold** type. This shows that the
word is listed in the glossary on page 46. The glossary gives a brief explanation of words which may
be new to you.

Contents

Introduction

This book tells the story of sailors and the sea. Two thirds of the surface of the earth is covered by the seas and the oceans. The land is broken up into masses. The large masses of land are called **continents**. The small ones are called islands.

When the first sailors went to sea, they did not know what they would find at the end of their journeys. There were no maps to help them. No one knew what lands lay beyond the **horizon**. Every journey was an adventure. People went to sea to find new places to live. They traded goods from their own countries with goods from others. Sometimes they just took what they found.

When they came home, they told stories about what they had seen. People began to know about the world. Sailors brought back new kinds of food and new ideas. They learned to find their way from one place to another by using the stars to guide them. They drew maps of where they had been.

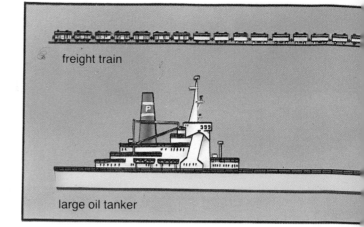

freight train

large oil tanker

▼ You can see a road and railroad built along the valley of the Rhine River in West Germany. Railroads, roads and rivers all carry people and goods.

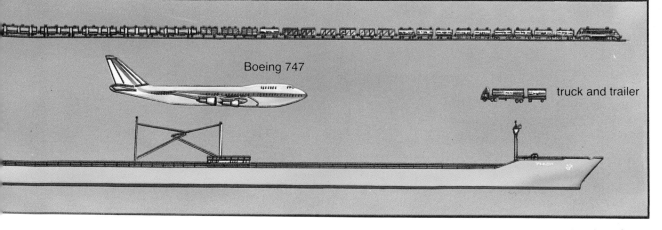

Boeing 747

truck and trailer

Sailing the Seas

Life has never been easy for sailors. Ships can be wrecked on rocky coasts or on rocks hidden under the water. In the oceans, large waves can swamp and sink smaller boats. Strong winds and gales can blow them off course. Without wind, however, sailing ships can be **becalmed**. They are unable to move. Ships without engines might be unable to sail on for weeks.

The earliest sailors used their muscles to paddle their boats along. Then they began to use sails to catch the wind. It is only in the past 150 years that engines have been used to do the work.

Now there are thousands of ships at sea. Some carry people. Others carry **cargo**. Although travel by sea is slower than by land or air, ships can carry heavier cargoes. They can also carry more people than airplanes or the longest train.

Moving Through Water

It is very hard work making a boat move through water. As a boat moves forward, the water in front of it slows it down. Because of this, the smallest boats and the largest ships all have pointed **bows**. This helps them to cut their way through the water. People have tried to make travel by water easier in many other ways.

▲ Ships carry more goods than trains but they are slower. Trains carry more than planes but they are slower. Planes carry more than heavy trucks and they are faster.

▼ Sailing boats are used for fun and for sport. They do not need engines. They use the power of the wind.

How It All Began

The first people to travel by water probably found out how to do so by accident. Perhaps they lived near a river. Someone may have seen a floating log and climbed on to it. Later, the people may have used the log to fish from or to cross a river.

The next step was to hollow out a log to make a simple boat. This could be done with flint tools or by fire. These boats were called **dugouts**. Another piece of wood was shaped to make a paddle.

Dugouts must have been heavy and difficult to handle. Soon, other kinds of boats were made. Smaller logs were tied together to make rafts. Rafts could be steered and pushed along with a pole long enough to reach the river bed.

The first people found that they could use a log to travel by water. They sat on the log and used a piece of wood to paddle the log along.

Floating

Have you ever wondered why some things float in water and some sink? If an object is made of something heavier than water, it will sink. If it is lighter, it will float. That is why a piece of iron or a stone will sink, but a piece of wood will float.

The first real boat was a long tree trunk with some of the wood carved or burnt out of it. This kind of boat is called a dugout canoe.

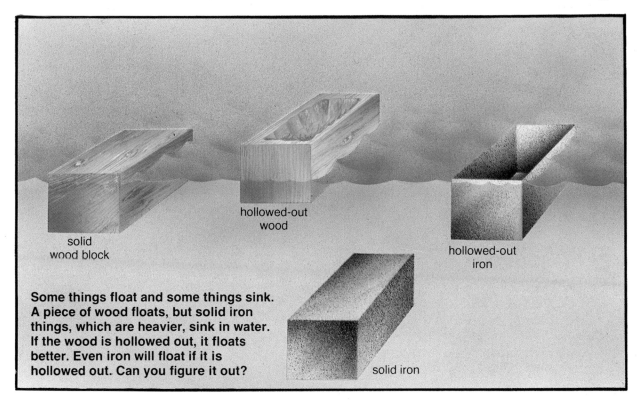

solid
wood block

hollowed-out
wood

hollowed-out
iron

solid iron

**Some things float and some things sink.
A piece of wood floats, but solid iron
things, which are heavier, sink in water.
If the wood is hollowed out, it floats
better. Even iron will float if it is
hollowed out. Can you figure it out?**

Anything put into water will take up some space. Because of this the water level rises. This is called **displacement**. When you get into the bath, your body displaces some of the water. Sit up in the bath and look at the water level. Now lie down. You will see that the water level has risen. If you have put too much water in the bath, some of it will overflow.

If you put a solid block of wood in water, it will float. Most of it, though, will be under the water. The wood displaces its own weight of water. If you hollow out the piece of wood to make a dugout, it will float higher in the water. There is less weight to be displaced.

Iron does not float. If a ship is built of thin sheets of iron, however, it does float. This is because it displaces only the weight of the thin sheets and this weight is spread over a large area of water. If a ship is filled with too much cargo, it will displace too much water and sink.

▼ **Fill a bowl with water right to the top. Now lower something into the water. The water overflows. It is displaced. Try this with something that floats, like an orange. The further things sink, the more water they displace.**

The Nile River

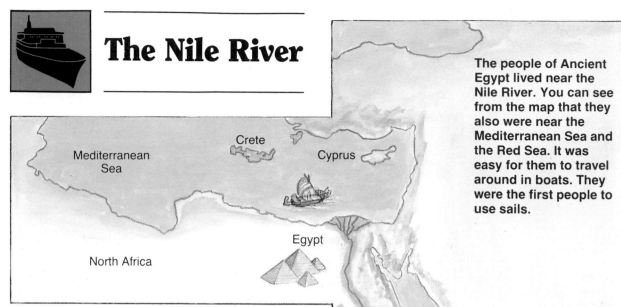

The people of Ancient Egypt lived near the Nile River. You can see from the map that they also were near the Mediterranean Sea and the Red Sea. It was easy for them to travel around in boats. They were the first people to use sails.

Historians feel that the first people to build real boats lived in Ancient Egypt. This was about 5,000 years ago. They lived near the banks of the Nile River. You can see that it was easy for them to travel from one place to another by water.

Their first boats were made of bundles of **reeds** tied together. They were small boats and could carry only one or two people. A paddle was used to move the boat through the water.

The Boat Builders

The Egyptians wanted to build larger boats. In order to do this, they needed a material that would be stronger than reeds. There were lots of small **acacia** trees in Egypt, but no large trees. At first, the Egyptians used the wood from acacia trees to build their boats. These boats were stronger and larger than those made of reeds, but still not large enough or strong enough. This was because the builders could only obtain short planks and a short **keel** from small trees. The keel is an unbroken beam of wood that goes along the length of the bottom of a boat. It gives the boat strength and acts like a human backbone.

8

► The Egyptians made their boats with short planks of wood. The boards were curved at both ends. While the boat was being built, the ends were tied together by a long rope. Then, the rope was tightened to give the boat strength.

The Egyptians were also the first people to use the wind to push their boats along. They grew cotton and wove it into **sailcloth**. Their boats had one large square sail. The sailors were able to turn the sail with ropes in order to catch the wind. If there was no wind, the sailors used paddles instead.

In order to steer, the Egyptians fixed a paddle to the back, or **stern**, of the boat. This paddle acted as a **rudder**. When the rudder was turned in one direction, the boat turned the same way.

Ships for Trading

About 4,000 years ago, the Egyptians were using their ships to take goods up and down the Nile River. Some sailors went further and took their ships to sea. They discovered other lands.

Egypt began to trade with other countries. Ships carried grain and cotton across the sea. They brought back jewels, spices, wood, and metal.

There was a great queen of Egypt whose name was Hatshepsut (*Hat-shep-sut*). She sent sailors to explore new lands and find treasure. They sailed down the Red Sea to the land we now call Ethiopia. They went across the Mediterranean Sea to the island of Crete. The sailors brought back gifts for the queen. They brought her cattle and monkeys, as well as jewels.

▼ Queen Hatshepsut's boats were large. Each boat had a mast and one large square sail. The mast was held in place by ropes. There was a large paddle at the stern. They used this paddle to steer the boat.

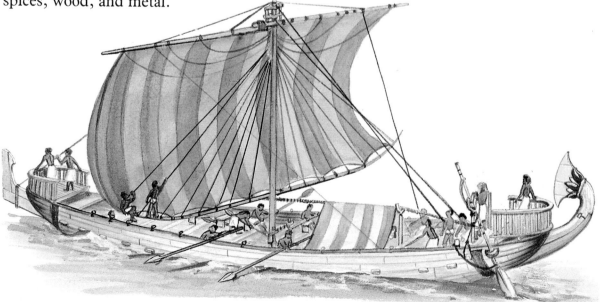

The Phoenicians

One of the lands Egyptian sailors went to was Phoenicia (*Fe-nish-ia*). This is now called Lebanon. The Phoenicians began to build ships of their own. They had tall **cedar** trees which they could use. Their ships had long, straight keels. These ships were strong and could sail in rough seas. They had large, square sails. On board also were teams of men with oars. On some ships there were two or three banks, or rows, of oarsmen, one bank above the other.

The Phoenicians built two kinds of ships.

They used **longships** for battle. These were long, narrow ships with **rams** at the bow. The rams were used to sink enemy ships. With their two or three banks of oarsmen, longships could travel fast. They were the first warships. Other countries soon began to build their own. The other kind of Phoenician ship was called the **round ship**

Phoenician longships traveled very fast. They had sails, but they also carried many oarsmen. You can see the two banks of oars and the oarsmen, one above the other.

because of its shape. It was wider and traveled more slowly. This kind of ship was used for carrying cargo.

The Phoenicians were brave warriors and sailors. They fought many sea battles around the Mediterranean Sea. They were also explorers. They sailed out of the Mediterranean into the Atlantic Ocean. They set up trading posts wherever they went. One of these was at Carthage in North Africa. Carthage became a great city. Ships from Phoenicia also went down the Red Sea and right around Africa. Others sailed to England and northern Europe.

Greek and Roman Ships

Phoenician sailors went to Greece and Rome. The Greeks and Romans copied their ships. Their longships were known as **galleys**. A Roman galley was like an improved Phoenician longship. The Romans put a second sail at the bow. They put a paddle on each side of the stern. This made it easier to steer. Just in front of the stern, they built a **deckhouse** on warships. This looked like a castle. The Romans conquered most of western Europe. They used their ships to bring goods and treasure back to Rome.

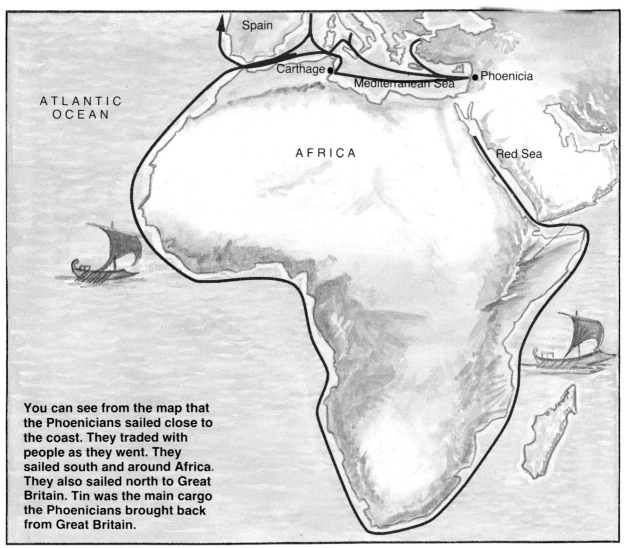

You can see from the map that the Phoenicians sailed close to the coast. They traded with people as they went. They sailed south and around Africa. They also sailed north to Great Britain. Tin was the main cargo the Phoenicians brought back from Great Britain.

The Vikings

The Vikings lived in northern Europe about 1,000 years ago. They were fierce warriors and good sailors. They loved the sea, and they enjoyed exploring new lands.

The Vikings found a new way to build ships. They used long planks of wood. Each plank overlapped the one below. This type of ship is called **clinker built**. We know exactly what Viking boats were like.

When a leader died, his ship was buried with him. Some of these Viking ships have been dug up and restored.

There were many different types of Viking ships. Short, wide ships were used to carry cargo. The Vikings built longships for fighting and exploring. Their longships were curved up at the bow and stern. There was often a **figurehead** on the bow. This was a carving of the head of a dragon or a snake.

▼ Viking longships were long and narrow. Each ship had one brightly colored sail. The Vikings stood up in their open boats when they rowed. Although they were not protected from the weather, the Vikings made voyages to Iceland and Greenland. They also traveled as far as North America in longships like this one.

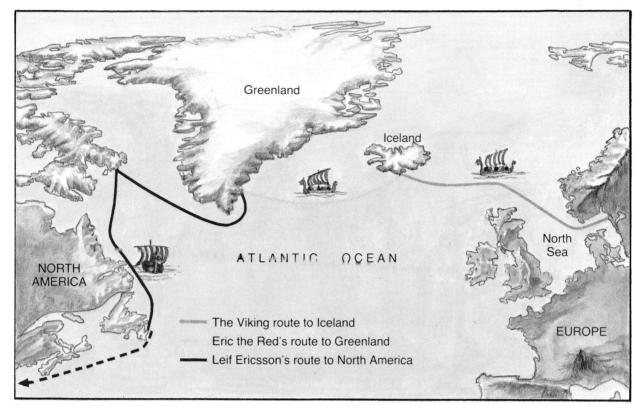

The Viking route to Iceland
Eric the Red's route to Greenland
Leif Ericsson's route to North America

▲ Nearly 1000 years ago, Leif Ericsson sailed on from Greenland. He found a place which he called Vinland. There were vines and grapes growing there. Some people think Vinland was near New England. He may have been the first person from Europe to discover America.

The biggest longships had up to 80 oarsmen. They had large, square sails in bright colors. Viking ships had one steering oar, or rudder. It was attached to the right side of the stern. This "stern board" gave sailors the word **starboard**. Starboard means the right-hand side of a ship. The sailor's word for the left-hand side is **port**. When longships were in port, they tied up on that side. This way they did not damage the rudder.

The Vikings sailed all around Europe. They went across the Baltic Sea to Russia. At first, they explored other lands. Later, Viking families settled in the lands they had visited.

Leif Ericsson

The Vikings also sailed west into the Atlantic Ocean. They discovered Iceland. Viking families settled there. Sailors went out from Iceland to look for other new lands.

One of the sailors was called Eric the Red. He sailed west from Iceland and found Greenland. Eric the Red settled in Greenland and had a son whose name was Leif Ericsson. Leif Ericsson became an explorer like his father.

One day, Leif Ericsson's ship was blown off course in a gale. The wind blew it westwards. He landed at a place where he saw grape vines growing. He called the new land Vinland because of the vines. Vinland may have been on the coast of New England, but we are not sure.

The Vikings did not settle in Vinland. It was another 400 years before sailors from Europe found America again.

Using the Wind

▶ The Arabs were the first people to use a lateen sail. This sail was in the shape of a triangle. A lateen sail works better than a square sail when the wind is blowing from the side. Arab dhows still use lateen sails today.

All the ships you have read about so far had square sails. Square sails worked well if there was a **following wind** from behind the ship. The sails were of no use if the wind was blowing from any other direction. That is why square-sailed ships needed oarsmen. The men provided the power to push the ship forward if the wind was not right. Arab seamen in the Red Sea and the Indian Ocean used another kind of sail. They sailed in light boats called **dhows**. These boats had one sail in the shape of a triangle. One side of the sail was fixed to the mast. The opposite corner was fixed to the side of the boat. The Romans copied this idea. They built boats with two or more triangular sails. These came to be called **lateen** sails.

Lateen sails were set along the length of the ship instead of across the width. Because of this, lateen sails were better than square sails when the wind was blowing across the ship. This was called a **beam wind**.

14

Catching the Wind

If a boat with lateen sails heads straight into the wind, the sails do not pick up any air. The boat will not move. Unlike square sails, however, lateen sails can be **trimmed**. This means moving them from side to side so that the wind catches them. The boat can go forward then by **tacking**. A boat makes a zig-zag course when it is tacking.

When a boat tacks, the sails are trimmed to catch the wind, first on one side and then on the other side. The boat can sail on either side of the wind. Tacking takes longer because the boat is not moving in a straight line, but the boat can move forward when sailing against the wind.

The Romans used ships with both kinds of sails. They had large, square sails for use in a following wind. They also had lateen sails for use when the wind was across or in front of them.

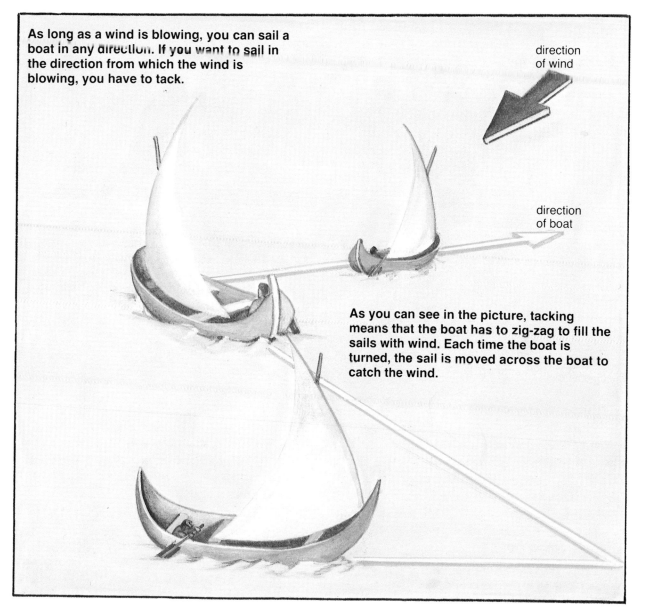

As long as a wind is blowing, you can sail a boat in any direction. If you want to sail in the direction from which the wind is blowing, you have to tack.

direction of wind

direction of boat

As you can see in the picture, tacking means that the boat has to zig-zag to fill the sails with wind. Each time the boat is turned, the sail is moved across the boat to catch the wind.

How Ships Changed

After the time of the Vikings, the boat-builders of the Mediterranean countries had new ideas. They added more masts and sails to give their ships extra speed. They used some square and some lateen sails. A rudder attached to the stern was used to steer, instead of a paddle. They made their ships out of stronger wood. These ships were safer in rough seas. Wooden "castles," or small towers, were built at the bow and stern. The deck at the bow of a ship is still called the fo'c'sle, or **forecastle**.

There were pirates at sea in those days. They attacked merchant ships to take their goods. Merchant ships, like warships, were given "castles" to protect the crew.

At first, warships fought by ramming each other. Sailors fought with **pikes** or poles if they were close enough. Later, around 1400, ships carried heavy guns. Special gun decks were built into warships. The guns were fired through gun ports – holes cut in the ship's sides. About this time, a **crowsnest** was fixed at the top of the **mainmast**. There, a lookout would keep watch for land, pirates, or enemy ships.

▲ Galleys like this one were used as warships in the Mediterranean Sea for many years. Sometimes, they had two square sails. There was a steering oar at the stern of the galley.

▲ The cog was a small merchant ship. The cog had "castles" to protect the crew.

► The Portuguese were great sailors and explorers. They built the first caravel. The first caravels had two square sails and one lateen sail.

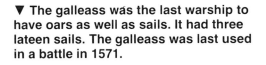

▼ The galleass was the last warship to have oars as well as sails. It had three lateen sails. The galleass was last used in a battle in 1571.

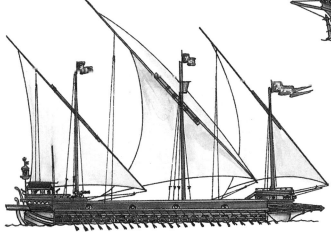

▲ Galleons stood high out of the water. They had large "castles" at the bow and at the stern. They carried heavy guns on three or more decks.

▼ Spanish sailors used their galleons as merchant ships as well as for war. Galleons were strong and safe for long ocean voyages.

▲ Carracks were very large ships. Some could carry several hundred passengers. Carracks were used as warships and as merchant ships.

Christopher Columbus

▼ Christopher Columbus set sail from Spain in 1492. He reached the West Indies after a voyage of 69 days. During the next 10 years, Columbus made three more journeys across the Atlantic Ocean to find a way through to the Indian Ocean.

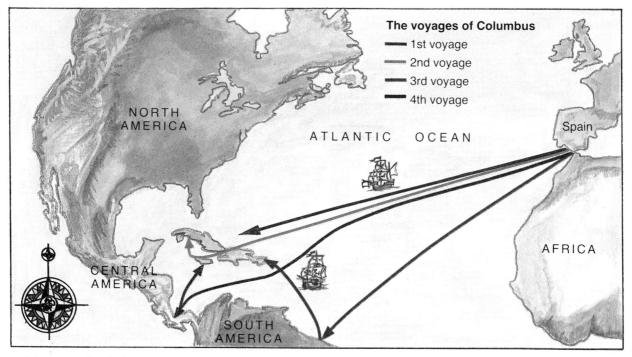

The voyages of Columbus
— 1st voyage
— 2nd voyage
— 3rd voyage
— 4th voyage

NORTH AMERICA

ATLANTIC OCEAN

Spain

CENTRAL AMERICA

AFRICA

SOUTH AMERICA

Many of the goods that people in Europe wanted came from Asia. Silk came from China, and spices came from India. They were brought by land. Explorers thought that if they sailed west from Europe, they would reach Asia more quickly. It would be easier to bring back goods by sea than by land.

Christopher Columbus was one man who thought this way. He was a sailor from Genoa in Italy. He studied books and maps and planned his **voyage**. However, he had no money to buy ships.

He went to Portugal to ask the king for help. The king would not help, so Columbus went to Spain. It took four years before the king of Spain said he would pay for the voyage.

Sailing West

In 1492, Columbus set sail. He had 88 men and three ships. He sailed in a **carrack** called the *Santa Maria*. The other two ships were **caravels**. These small, fast sailing ships were named the *Pinta* and the *Nina*. They sailed west across the Atlantic.

▼ The *Santa Maria* was only about 96 feet long. A large oil tanker today is about ten times as long.

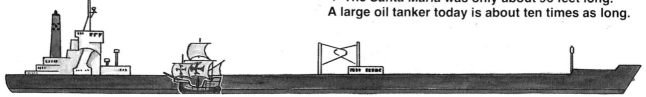

After six weeks, they had seen no land. The sailors began to be afraid. How would they get back home? Would their voyage ever end? But Columbus took no notice. "Sail on!" he ordered.

Then, when the sailors had been at sea for two months, they saw the branch of a tree floating in the water. Land must be near. The next night, a lookout in the crowsnest of the *Nina* called, "Land ahoy!" The long voyage was over.

Columbus thought it must be India. But it was not. It was the island of San Salvador in the Bahamas. Columbus landed there. Then, he explored some of the other islands nearby. He called them the Indies because he thought they were part of India. We call them the West Indies to this day.

Later Voyages

Columbus sailed across the Atlantic four times. He put settlers on some of the islands in the West Indies. On his third voyage, he found South America. On his fourth, he got as far as Panama. He was still sure that he was close to India and that if he sailed on, he would get there. However, he was thousands of miles away. There was no way through from the Atlantic to the Pacific. Columbus had found Central America, but he still thought he had found a part of Asia.

▼ The *Santa Maria* carried a crew of 52 men. This picture shows a model of the ship. As well as a square mainsail, the *Santa Maria* carried a smaller topsail.

Around the World

Columbus was just one of the men who tried to find a way to Asia by sailing west. Another was John Cabot. He was from Genoa like Columbus. In 1497, he set sail from England. There were only 18 men on one small carrack. After 53 days, he sighted land. He was sure he had reached China, but he was wrong, too. He landed at Cape Breton Island on the east coast of Canada.

Next year, he sailed west again. He went up the coast of Labrador. Then he sailed south as far as Chesapeake Bay. Supplies, however, ran short, and he had to go back to England. John Cabot was the first explorer since the Vikings to land on the mainland of North America.

East and West

At this time, Spain and Portugal had the best ships. They sent sailors from Europe to explore other lands. Amerigo Vespucci, an Italian, led several explorations for Spain and Portugal. In 1501, he sailed west and discovered South America, but he did not land there. Vespucci realized that America was not part of Asia. It was a "new" continent. America is named after him.

Other sailors went east from Europe. Vasco da Gama was from Portugal. He set out to sail to India. He went around South Africa and crossed the Indian Ocean. In 1498, he reached India. He was the first European to get there by sea.

▼ The map shows the routes of the main sea voyages made by six of the great explorers. Columbus discovered the West Indies. Magellan was the first explorer to sail around the world. Sir Francis Drake made the same voyage around the world 58 years later.

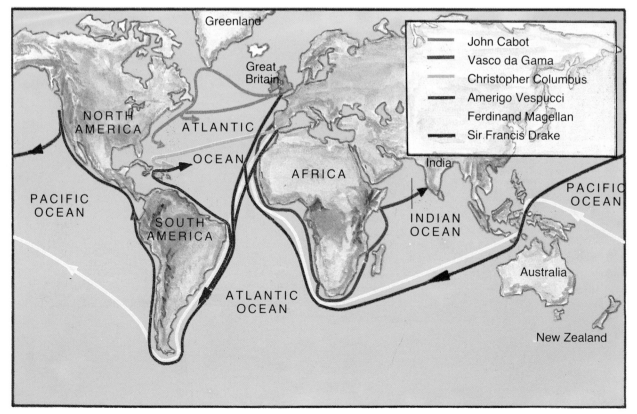

▲ This old picture shows Magellan's ships passing through the channel of water between the Atlantic and Pacific Oceans. It was named the Magellan Straits after him.

▼ Sir Francis Drake was the first Englishman to sail around the world. He sailed from England in his ship, the *Golden Hind*, in 1577. He arrived home three years later in 1580.

Ferdinand Magellan

Ferdinand Magellan was the explorer whose crew sailed around the world. He came from Portugal. He wanted to try to find a westward route to China. The king of Portugal would not help, but the king of Spain gave him five ships.

The five ships set sail in 1519. They sailed west to Brazil. Then they went south. It was a terrible voyage. The men quarreled and fought. Food was short. One ship was wrecked, and another went home. Still Magellan went on. At last, he sailed around Cape Horn into the calm Pacific Ocean.

There was more trouble to come. The men saw no land for months. They were short of food and water. Some of the sailors died. They found an island called Macta and landed on it. Magellan was killed in a fight. One of his captains finally reached home with only one ship and 17 men.

Australasia

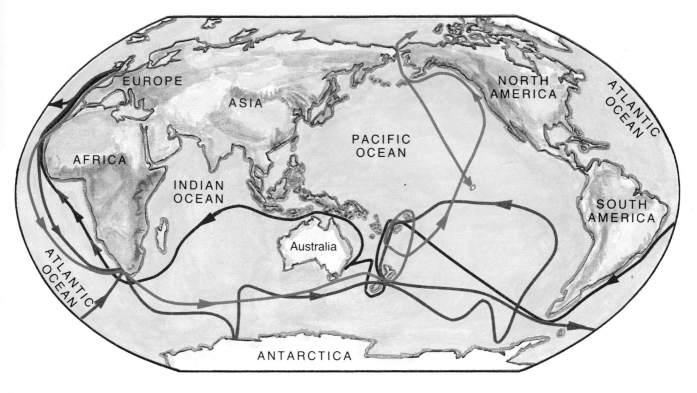

People had sailed west from Europe and found America. Some thought that there was another continent in the south. They called it the "South Land."

A Dutch sailor, Abel Tasman, set out to find it. In 1642, he discovered Tasmania and New Zealand. Two years later, he found the north coast of Australia. He thought these were all parts of the South Land. But he could not make them fit together into a map. So far, the map of the South Land showed just a few bits of coast.

James Cook

In 1768, an English sailor set out to find out more about the South Land. His name was James Cook. He joined the navy as a seaman. Then he worked his way up to command his own ship. He was an expert at making **charts**, which are the maps that sailors use.

Cook did not want to find gold or treasure. He wanted to make a chart of the South Land, if he could find it. He took two scientists with him. His ship was a converted coal ship called the *Endeavour*.

Cook sailed west across the Atlantic and around Cape Horn. He explored the South Sea island of Tahiti. Then he sailed south to look for the South Land. He did not find it. So he sailed on to New Zealand. He made a chart of the coast there.

He decided to sail west and reach home that way. He came to the east coast of Australia. His men landed in a place where

22

there were large numbers of wild flowers. They decided to call it Botany Bay. **Botany** is the science which deals with flowers. This was the first landing in Australia by people from Europe.

Cook set sail on his last voyage in 1776. He sailed around Africa and across the Indian Ocean. He went across the Pacific. When he reached the coast of North America, he turned north. There is a **channel** between Asia and America. It is called the Bering Strait. Cook sailed up this channel. Soon, he could go no further. In front of the ship was a wall of ice. There was no way through. He returned to Hawaii in the Pacific Ocean.

The people who lived there had been friendly on Cook's previous visit. This time they stole a small boat. He tried to punish them, and they started fighting. During this fight, six chiefs were killed, and James Cook was stabbed to death.

▲ Captain James Cook, who was born in 1728 and died in 1779.

▼ James Cook chose the *Endeavour* for his voyage around the world, because it was a very strong ship. At one time, the *Endeavour* had been used for carrying coal. Two lower decks were put in. You can see that the crew lived on the first deck. Food and drink were stored on the second deck.

Clipper Ships

Settlers from Europe went to live in the "new lands" that had been discovered. They hoped to find freedom and make a better life for themselves and their families. Many of them became farmers.

Ships were needed to take the settlers out and bring back the goods they produced. A new kind of fast ship was built for this trade. It was called a **clipper**. The first clipper was built in 1832. She was called the *Ann McKim*. She sailed between America and China.

Clippers were long and narrow. They had sharp, pointed bows which cut through the waves. Each of their three tall masts had up to six sails. There were deep **holds** for the passengers or cargo. Clippers made regular trips across the Atlantic. They took passengers westwards. On the way back, they carried cargo. They were given the job of carrying mail because they were so fast.

▲ This ship, the *Pride of Baltimore*, is a clipper.

▼ The *Ann McKim* was the first Baltimore clipper. She was built in 1832 for a local merchant, Isaac McKim, and was named after his wife.

The Rush for Gold

In 1849, gold was found in California. People hurried there to join in the "gold rush." The quickest way from the east coast of America was by sea. A clipper took three months to sail from New York around Cape Horn. No one had traveled so fast by sea before. Then, there was a gold rush in Australia. Thousands of people sailed to Australia by clipper from Europe.

The Tea Races

Steamships were soon to take over the passenger and mail trade. Clippers, however, went on being used for cargo. Some goods spoil if they spend too long on their way to the stores. One of these goods is tea. It dries out and loses its flavor if it is kept in boxes for very long.

Fast ships were needed to bring the new crop of tea from China to London. The clipper ships were just right for the job. Steamships would have had to stop to take on coal or wood. Clippers could sail all the way without stopping.

Every year, there was a race to bring the first new crop of tea to London. Tea merchants gave a prize to the fastest clipper. The *Cutty Sark* was one of the most famous tea clippers. It once sailed 363 miles in one day. No other clipper ever beat this record. Later, the *Cutty Sark* brought wool from Australia. It took 69 days. The usual time was 100 days.

▶ The *Cutty Sark* was a British tea clipper that was built in 1869. She is now a museum ship at Greenwich, near London. In this picture, you can see the full cargo of tea stored below deck.

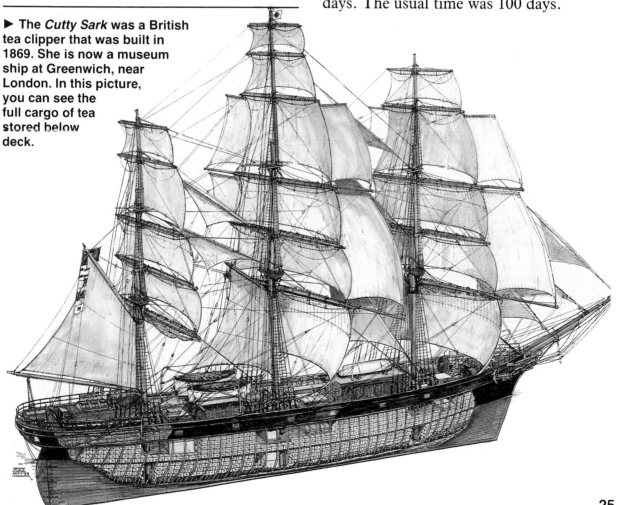

The Coming of Steam

The steam engine was invented around 1770. It was not long before someone thought of using a steam engine to drive a ship. The first steamships were used on rivers.

The steam in a steam engine is made by boiling water. Wood or coal is needed to stoke the fire. The first steamships could not go very far without stopping for more fuel. They could not carry enough fuel to take them across the Atlantic Ocean.

The First Steamships

An American named John Fitch ran the first steamship service in 1790. It was on the Delaware River. His ship, called the *Experiment*, had a number of large oars at the stern. They were driven back and forth by a steam engine. However, John Fitch lost money and had to stop this service.

▲ John Fitch's steamboat, *Experiment*, was driven by three large oars at the stern.

Another American, Robert Fulton, built a ship called the *Clermont*. This ship had two paddle wheels, one on each side of the **hull**, like the wheels of a water mill. The engine pushed the wheels around. When the paddles went into the water, they drove the ship forward.

In 1807, Robert Fulton ran a service between New York and Albany.

The *Clermont* made her first journey in 1807. She steamed up the Hudson River from New York to Albany and back in 62 hours. This was a distance of about 240 miles.

The *Clermont* steamed at about the same speed as a person can walk. It could carry about 100 people.

At that time in America, there were no railroads. The highways were poor, but there were many rivers. The best way to travel a long distance was by river. This was why so many steamships were built in America. By 1822, there were 35 steamers on the Mississippi alone.

Sternwheelers

Most paddle steamers had a wheel on each side of the hull. However, a new type of ship was built on the Mississippi. It was called a **sternwheeler**. It had one large

▲ The sternwheeler, *Delta Queen*, at work on the Mississippi River near Alabama. The man standing at the stern looks very small next to the huge paddle wheel.

paddle wheel at the stern. Only a small part of the wheel went into the water. Because of this, sternwheelers could be used in shallow waters.

These boats carried people, cargo, and mail up and down the great rivers of North America. They helped to open up the country. There are still some sternwheelers on American rivers today. Of course, it is quicker to travel by road or air, but it is much more fun to go by river.

Paddles and Propellers

The Atlantic was first crossed by an American steamship in 1819. The ship was the *Savannah*. She was a sailing ship equipped with paddles. She took 21 days to sail from New York to Liverpool, but she used her sails most of the way. The first ship to steam all the way was the *Royal William*. She steamed from Canada to England in 1823.

The first ocean steamships had sails as well as engines. Sails were used if the engines broke down or the ships ran out of fuel. So much fuel was needed that there was little room for cargo or passengers. Steamships lost money on the Atlantic run. Sailing ships were less expensive to operate.

In 1838, a race was planned between two British steamships across the Atlantic Ocean. One of the ships was not ready in time for the race. The *Sirius* took part instead. Although she was not built to race across the Atlantic, she did very well. The *Sirius* took 18 days to steam from Liverpool to New York. She did not use her sails at all. On the way, the *Sirius* ran out of coal. Cabin doors, furniture, planks and one mast were used as fuel to keep her going. The other ship was the *Great Western*. She was built to cross the Atlantic Ocean. The *Great Western* made the crossing in 15 days and still had plenty of coal left at the end of the journey.

The paddle-steamer *Britannia*.

Samuel Cunard

One man found a way of making money with steam. He was Samuel Cunard. He had owned a share in the *Royal William*. Now he started a company on his own. He won the **contract** to carry mail between Britain and Canada. Mail did not take up much space.

Cunard built four paddle steamers for the job. The first was the *Britannia*. Her first voyage was in July, 1840. She took just 14 days to steam from England to Canada. This was a record. Cunard's company became one of the great Atlantic shipping lines.

Brunel

Isambard Kingdom Brunel was a British **engineer**. He had built the *Great Western*. She was the first steamship to provide a regular service across the Atlantic. Now, he decided to build a larger ship. She was called the *Great Britain*. She was made of iron, and she was the biggest ship ever built up to that time. The *Great Britain* was the first ocean steamship to have a **propeller** instead of paddles. There were also six masts of sails.

Sadly, she ran aground on her fifth voyage. Brunel sold her. After many adventures, she ended up as a wreck in the Falkland Islands. In 1970, she was brought back to Britain, and she is now on show in Bristol. She lies in the same dock where she was built in 1843.

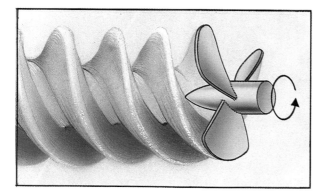

◄ The ship's engine makes the propeller turn around. As the propeller turns, its curved blades "bite" into the water. They force the water backwards, so that the ship moves forwards. The first propellers had two very long blades. They often broke. Today, propellers have three, four, or more very strong blades.

Passage to America

In the 1800's, millions of people left Europe to live in North America. Most of them were poor. They had just enough money to pay for their tickets.

This was good business for ship owners. All kinds of ships – steam, sail, large and small – were used. They carried as many passengers as they could.

A few rich people had cabins. The rest of the passengers lived and slept close together in the holds. It was a hard voyage. Ships **pitched** and **rolled** in the rough seas. Waves crashed over the decks. Passengers had to stay below deck. They each had about 18 inches of space to live and sleep in. They lay in bunks, one row above the other. They had to cook their own food. They were often too seasick to eat anything.

Seven million **emigrants** crossed the Atlantic like this. Some never reached the end of the voyage. Many ships sank in the storms. Sometimes, people died of sickness on the way.

The emigrants traveled below deck. They were crowded together like cattle.

Life on board ship was no better for the crew. They had very little space to live in, and their food was poor. Captains wanted to cross the Atlantic as fast as they could. They took risks with their ships. At the end of the trip, some captains would often try to cheat the crew out of their pay.

The Cabin Trade

Not everyone who crossed the Atlantic was poor. Not everyone was an emigrant. More and more people went to see their families or travel on business.

The voyage was no safer for them than for the poor. There was no hope for anyone if a ship went down in the middle of the ocean, but people who had cabins had a little more comfort. Their food was cooked for them. They had more room to sleep and to move around.

There were separate sleeping cabins for men and women. In the daytime, they used the space between decks. They would read, talk, or play cards, but they would all be looking forward to the end of the voyage. Crossing the Atlantic was no fun for them.

Rich people traveled in cabins or in open saloons like this.

Ocean Liners

In 1894, a British engineer, Charles Parsons, built a new kind of steamship engine. It was called a steam **turbine**. The steam drove a set of blades around and around. The blades were attached to the **propeller shaft**. When the shaft turned, so did the propeller.

Ships with turbines used less fuel and went faster. Parsons' turbine ship was called the *Turbinia*. It was a small boat, but it went at about 35 mph.

The first steam turbine ship crossed the Atlantic in 1904. She was called the *Virginian*. Soon, all the Atlantic shipping lines started to build bigger and faster turbine ships.

▼ In 1938, the *Queen Mary* crossed the Atlantic Ocean in 3 days, 20 hours, and 42 minutes. Her average speed was over 36 mph.

These new ocean **liners** were like huge hotels on water. They had ballrooms, swimming pools, shops, and restaurants. There were dances, shows, and concerts to help pass the time. The great days of ocean travel had arrived.

The Blue Riband

The United States and many European countries had liners on the Atlantic run. They competed with each other to make the crossing in the shortest time. The fastest ship won the Blue Riband of the Atlantic.

In 1907 the Blue Riband was won by a Cunard ship. She was the *Mauretania*. She held the record for 22 years. Then, it went to Germany, and afterwards to France.

The *Queen Mary* was a new Cunard ship. She made her **maiden voyage** in 1936. She crossed the Atlantic in under four days and won the Blue Riband. In 1952, the prize was won by a new US liner, the *United States*. She crossed in ten hours less than the *Queen Mary* at a speed of 41 mph.

▲ Cunard's liner, *Queen Elizabeth II* was launched in 1967. The QE2 is now a luxury cruise liner and carries 2,000 passengers.

Cruise Liners

Forty years ago, there were 60 liners on the Atlantic run. Now, there are none. Ship owners, however, have found a new way to use their ships. They use them for cruises, which are really "vacations at sea." Cruise ships are even more like hotels than the Atlantic liners used to be.

If you have the time and the money, you can cruise around the world. If you do not have time you can take a short cruise of a few days. Cruise liners often travel fast at night. This way, the passengers can go ashore each day at a new port.

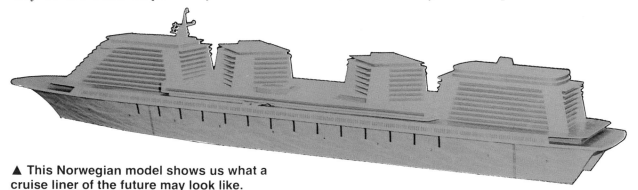

▲ This Norwegian model shows us what a cruise liner of the future may look like.

The Busy Seas

There are many thousands of ships at work throughout the world. Most of them are **freighters**. These are ships that mainly carry cargo. Over half of them carry a mixture of goods. They might carry machines, timber, wheat, or fruit. There may be up to four decks in the hold of a freighter. These decks are divided by steel walls called **bulkheads**. The divisions make it easier to load and unload a ship with cargo for different places. Some freighters carry a few passengers as well as cargo.

▲ "Roro" ferries are built to carry cars and trucks on short sea routes or across wide rivers. Roro stands for "roll on, roll off." These ferry boats have a bow and a stern that can open up to make a ramp. People can drive cars and trucks straight on board. They can drive off again at the end of the voyage. This means that the ferry boats can be loaded and unloaded very quickly. A large ferry boat can carry 350 cars or about 60 large trucks. Before roro ferries were used, cars and trucks had to be loaded and unloaded by a crane.

◄ The trailer of a milk carrier is being unloaded by a crane. This harbor is in Miami, Florida.

Loading and Unloading

It is important to load and unload quickly when a ship is in port. A cargo ship earns money only when it is on the move. Many of these ships have deck cranes called **derricks**. These are used to lift the cargo out of the hold.

Ships are loaded with great care. Heavy freight must be spread evenly. Ships must not be overloaded. On the side of every ship there is a painted line called the **Plimsoll line**. When the water level touches the line, it shows that the ship is fully loaded.

The smallest cargo ships are called **coasters**. These are the small delivery trucks of the sea. They can use almost any port. They go from one port to another and pick up any cargo they can. Coasters stay fairly close to the land. Usually, they have a crew of only three or four people.

▲ Freighters are docked at Kowloon Harbor, Hong Kong. The ship with the yellow tunnel is empty. She is high out of the water. The river boats alongside have cargo for loading. There are also containers on the dockside.

Coming into Harbor

Ships do not come into harbor like automobiles driving into a parking lot. They cannot stop quickly. They do not turn easily. Docking a ship is a skilled job.

It is usually the job of the harbor **pilot**. He is a captain who knows the harbor well. He goes out to meet the ship in a pilot boat. This is a small motor boat. He joins the captain on the **bridge** and guides the ship into the harbor.

When the ship sails again, it may be towed out of the harbor by tugs. These are small ships with very powerful engines. They pull the ship out to the open sea.

Inland Waterways

Not all travel by water is across the sea. Boats travel inland, too. Sometimes they use **canals** made by people. Sometimes they use wide rivers. Rivers and canals used for shipping are called **inland waterways**.

Canals do not all pass over flat country. Boats using canals may have to cross high ground. When they do this, they must go through **locks**. Then, they can move from one level to another. A boat going "uphill" goes into the lock. The gates close behind it. Water is pumped into the lock until it is at the higher level. Then the gates in front are opened and the boat can move on.

Most of the cargo on inland waterways is carried by **barge**. A barge is a flat-bottomed boat specially built for inland waterways. Some have engines, but most do not. Those without engines are called **dumb barges**. Sometimes they are towed by a tug. Sometimes push-boats are used to push a string of dumb barges.

▼ How locks work

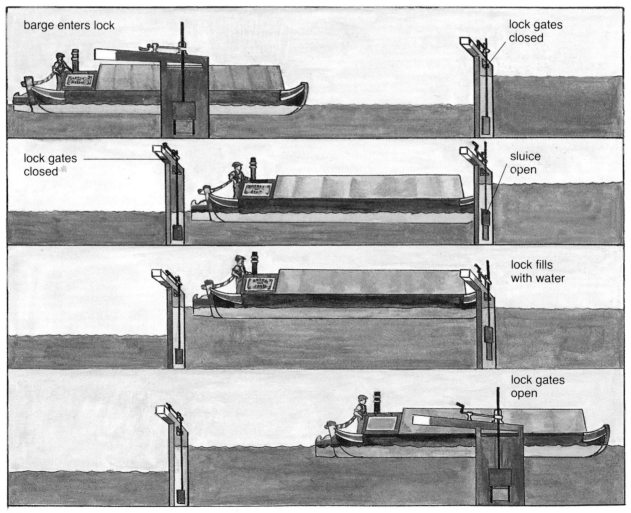

barge enters lock

lock gates closed

lock gates closed

sluice open

lock fills with water

lock gates open

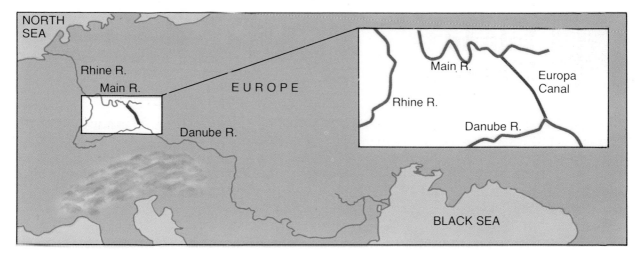

▲ The Europa Canal will be finished soon. The Main and the Danube Rivers will be joined by a canal. Then, it will be possible to travel by water all the way from the North Sea to the Black Sea.

▼ The map shows the world's largest inland waterway system. The Missouri joins the Mississippi at St Louis. The length of these two rivers together is 3,760 miles.

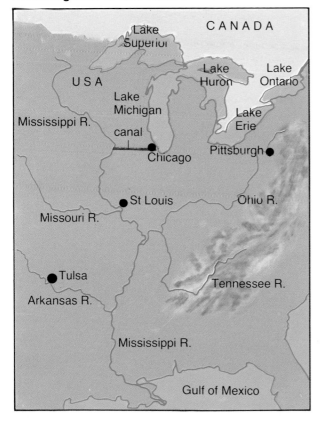

The Europa Canal

The Rhine, the Main and the Danube are three of Europe's longest rivers. The Rhine and the Main empty into the North Sea and the Danube empties into the Black Sea. They have been used as inland waterways for many years. However, there is a strip of land between the Main and the Danube. It is about 100 miles long. The plan is to dig a canal through this strip. Then, the rivers can be used all the way from the Netherlands to southern Russia. The first part of the route was opened in 1970.

The Mississippi

The Mississippi is the longest river in the United States. It flows south to the Gulf of Mexico. On the way, it is joined by other large rivers. They make up the world's largest inland waterway system.

Goods come from Tulsa in the west and Pittsburgh in the east. A canal links the Mississippi with Chicago. River travel is slow, but it is cheaper than road, rail, or air.

The Mississippi is so wide that barges are tied together to make rafts. There may be as many as 40 barges in one raft. Then, the raft is pushed along by a push-boat at the back.

The Great Canals

There is a thin strip of land separating the Red Sea from the Mediterranean. It is only 100 miles wide. At one time, goods brought by sea from Asia had to be unloaded at the northern end of the Red Sea. Camels then carried the goods north to Port Said in Egypt. From there, ships sailed across the Mediterranean to Europe. This took a lot of time, but it was easier and quicker than sailing all the way around Africa.

The Suez Canal

In 1859, it was decided to build a canal, or channel, along the old camel route. This was a huge task. The canal would link the Red Sea with the Mediterranean. The journey from Asia to Europe would be much quicker. A French engineer, Ferdinand de Lesseps, was in charge of the work. The work took much longer than he had expected. Britain and France had to give more money so that the work could go on.

Ten years later, the Suez Canal opened. A great fleet of 68 ships steamed through it. The leading ship was French. Flags flew and bands played. There were parties and fireworks.

You can see that the Suez Canal was dug out of the desert. The canal, which is 101 miles long, goes from Port Said to Suez.

The Panama Canal

A narrow strip of land joins North and South America at Panama. Before the canal was dug, ships had to sail around South America to get from the Atlantic to the Pacific Ocean. In the 1880s, de Lesseps started work on the canal, but he ran out of money. It was completed by American engineers in 1915. The Panama Canal is 42 miles long.

The St. Lawrence Seaway

The five Great Lakes of North America lie between the United States and Canada. All the water from these lakes flows out into the Atlantic Ocean along the St. Lawrence River. On the way, the water goes through rapids and over waterfalls. At one time, ships could use only some parts of the waterway.

The United States and Canada worked together to build larger locks and new canals. In 1959, the work was completed. The St. Lawrence Seaway is made up of lakes, canals, and locks on its journey to the sea. It stretches over about 2,300 miles from Thunder Bay, Lake Superior, to the Atlantic Ocean. All but the largest ships can use this seaway.

▲ Ships cannot use their engines in the locks on the Panama Canal. Electric engines are used to tow the ships through each lock. You can see the rails and the engine on the left-hand side of the lock.

During the winter months, parts of the seaway are frozen over. For the rest of the year, ships sail back and forth all the time. They carry grain, iron ore, and other goods to Europe and the rest of the world.

▶ The St. Lawrence Seaway is a great water highway linking the Great Lakes with the Atlantic Ocean. Large bulk cargo ships load up at Thunder Bay, Lake Superior, and at other ports on the Great Lakes. They carry grain and iron ore along the seaway. When they reach the Atlantic Ocean, the ships go to countries all over the world.

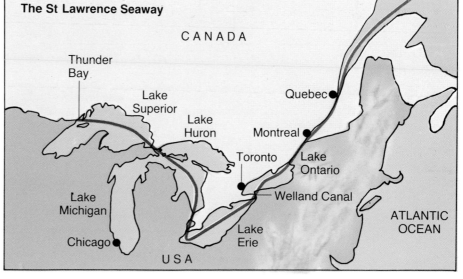

The St Lawrence Seaway

CANADA

Thunder Bay

Lake Superior

Lake Huron

Quebec

Montreal

Toronto

Lake Ontario

Welland Canal

Lake Michigan

Chicago

Lake Erie

USA

ATLANTIC OCEAN

Giant Carriers

Loading and unloading a cargo ship must be done quickly. The faster this work can be done, the sooner the ship can set off on its next voyage. Many ships are built to carry just one type of cargo. It might be grain, or sugar, or coal. These ships are called **bulk carriers**. They carry their cargo loose in their holds.

Oil Tankers

Tankers are specially built to carry oil and liquid fuels. Tankers are long, low ships with engines at their sterns. The rest of the space is taken up with oil tanks. The largest tankers can carry over 350,000 tons of oil. They can be more than 900 ft. long. Sometimes the crew use bicycles to get from one end to the other. Walking takes too long.

Although oil tankers are very large, they have small crews. Each crew member, however, is highly trained. They have to maintain safety. Oil burns easily. There is always a risk of fire. Because they are so large, tankers take a long time to slow down or alter course. They have computers to help them steer.

Like all ships, tankers sometimes have accidents at sea. When they do, oil may be spilled. This **pollutes** the sea. As a result, the oil can kill birds and fish. The oil may be swept ashore by the sea. When this happens, it spoils the beaches for the people who use them.

Container Ships

Another kind of ship is built to carry cargo in **containers**. These are very large metal boxes. Containers are all the same shape and size, so they fit neatly into the ship's hold. Some are stacked on deck. The first container ship went to sea in 1964.

Containers are filled at a factory. Then, they are taken to the port by road or rail. Containers are quicker and easier to load than bulk cargo. The containers can carry liquids as well as solid cargo. Liquids are carried in large plastic bags inside the containers.

Special ports have been built to handle these ships. They are called **container terminals**.

◄ The *British Trent* is owned by the British Petroleum (BP) Oil Company. She is a large tanker that carries oil.

► On the right, you can see a ship being unloaded at a container terminal. The containers are all the same size. They fit easily on top of each other. They can be put in the hold and on the deck of a container ship.

Safety at Sea

One night in 1912, a liner was steaming across the Atlantic from Southampton to New York. It was her maiden voyage. She was the largest ship at sea at that time. There were over 2,200 passengers and crew on board. The ship's name was the *Titanic*.

In the spring, icebergs float down to the Atlantic from the north. The *Titanic* hit an iceberg and she sank. About 1,500 people were drowned.

There were not enough lifeboats on the *Titanic*. Even if all the boats had been full, only half the people on board could have been saved.

It was the worst sea disaster ever. After this accident the safety rules at sea were changed. Now, ships must have lifeboats or life rafts for all the people on board.

The *Titanic* could have steered clear of the iceberg if the crew had known where the iceberg was. After the sinking, a **patrol** was set up to watch for icebergs and report them. This is done today by **satellites**.

Radar

Many things have changed since those days. Now, all ships have **radar**. Radar shows a picture of the sea around the ship. It shows the possible dangers. These could be other ships, icebergs, rocks, or the coast. Radar goes on working at night and in the fog.

Lights and Signals

Some stretches of water are very busy. One of these is the English Channel between France and England. In these places, ships have to keep in shipping lanes. The lanes are marked by **buoys** which send out radio and radar signals. Lightships and lighthouses also help to guide ships through dangerous waters. They have flashing lights and foghorns as well as radio and radar.

◄ In this picture, a ship's officer is looking at the radar screen. You can see that it is like a round TV screen. It works both night and day. The radar screen lights up to show the position of other ships, rocks, and land. The officer can tell by looking at the screen how far away these objects are from his ship. He can change course or slow the ship down to avoid hitting them.

Sea Rescue

Near the coast, there are special services to help ships in trouble. In the US, boats from the Coastguard Service patrol these coastal waters. There are also coastguard stations on shore. They have rescue boats. In Britain, the lifeboat service keeps rescue boats at shore stations ready for any **emergency**.

Helicopters are often used for sea rescue work. The helicopter crew lowers ropes to pick people out of the water. Sometimes, the helicopters are used to pick up sick people from ships at sea.

◄ This is a lighthouse in Maine. Ships at sea can figure out where they are when they see the light.

▼ This British lifeboat has been specially built. It does not sink if it turns over in a stormy sea.

New Kinds of Ships

The ships of today are quite different from those of 100 years ago. They are much larger and their engines are more powerful. They use oil as a fuel instead of coal. What about the future? Are there likely to be more changes?

Shipbuilders are trying out new ideas all the time. In 1958, the United States built a cargo ship driven by **nuclear power**. It was called the *Savannah* and could travel for three years without refuelling. However, the ship cost too much and no more were built.

The Japanese have gone back to an old idea. They have fitted an oil tanker with sails. Like the early steamers, it has engines as well. The sails are used only when the wind is right. They are controlled by a computer.

Even the fastest ships are slow compared with land or air travel. Ships cannot go much faster than 35 mph. This is because they have to force their way through water. If they can skim over the top of the water instead of through it, they can go much faster.

Hydrofoils

The **hydrofoil** has **foils** beneath the **hull**. They are like small aircraft wings, and they work in the same way. They are curved on top and flat underneath. As the hydrofoil gathers speed, the foils lift the boat out of the water, and it skims along the surface.

▼ This is a hydrofoil made by Boeing. As it gathers speed, the foils make it lift above the surface of the water.

The British hovercraft is starting on its journey. Air is pumped down below the hovercraft. This lifts it above the water. Four giant propellers drive it forward. The hovercraft can skim over the waves like a very low-flying plane. It can move over land as well as over water.

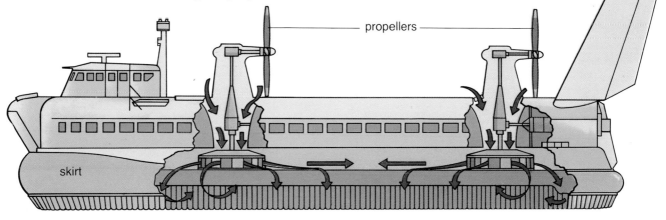

propellers

skirt

Hovercraft

The **hovercraft** floats on a cushion of air which lifts it above the water. Large pumps suck in air and pump it down to the **hull**. There, it is kept in place by a plastic or rubber "skirt." The air cannot escape and it makes a cushion. The hovercraft is driven forward by propellers which spin in the air like aircraft propellers.

Hydrofoils and hovercraft can go two or three times faster than ships. However, they can only be used in calm seas. In rough seas, they are easily damaged or overturned. Also, they give a bumpy and noisy ride. Maybe these problems will be solved some day. Then, giant hydrofoils and hovercraft may be used on the oceans.

Glossary

acacia: the name of a type of small tree and shrub found in warm countries.

barge: a flat-bottomed boat built to carry cargo on rivers and canals.

beam wind: a wind blowing across a ship as it moves forward.

becalmed: unable to move at sea because there is no wind.

botany: the study of plants.

bow: the front end of a boat or ship.

bridge: the raised section from which the captain controls the ship.

bulk carrier: a large ship which carries a loose dry cargo, like grain.

bulkheads: the steel walls which divide up the decks of a ship.

buoy: a floating marker attached to the bottom of the sea by a chain, which shows shipping lanes or warns of sunken wrecks or hidden rocks.

canal: a water channel built by people across land to connect two stretches of water.

caravel: a light, fast ship which originally had two square sails and one lateen sail at the stern.

cargo: goods carried by a ship.

carrack: a large, three-masted trading ship.

cedar: a kind of large evergreen tree whose wood was used for shipbuilding.

channel: a narrow stretch of water which is deep enough for ships to use.

charts: maps used by sailors.

clinker built: a method of building the hull or shell of a ship in which each plank of wood overlaps the one below it.

clipper: a long, narrow sailing ship built for speed. Clippers carried people and goods over long distances.

coaster: a small goods ship used for short voyages near the coast.

container: a large metal box for carrying goods.

container terminal: a port or part of a port where containers are loaded and unloaded.

continent: one of the large masses of land on earth. There are seven continents.

contract: a written agreement. Contracts are usually made by people in business.

crowsnest: a lookout position at the top of the mainmast. From the crowsnest a sailor can see land or ships that are far away.

deckhouse: a building on deck to protect the crew. It is usually near the stern.

derrick: a crane on the deck of a ship which is used to lift cargo in and out of the hold.

dhow: an Arab boat with one lateen sail.

displacement: the amount of water forced out of place when an object is put into the water.

dugout: a simple boat made by hollowing out a tree trunk.

dumb barge: a flat-bottomed boat, without an engine, which is built to carry cargo on rivers and canals. Dumb barges are often pulled or pushed by barges with engines or by tugs.

emergency: an unexpected danger.

emigrant: a person who moves from the country where they were born to live in another country.

engineer: a person who works or takes care of engines, or who builds large works such as canals, dams, and bridges.

figurehead: a carved wooden figure attached to the bow of a ship.

foil: a thin metal strip which is shaped like a ski or a fin of a fish.

following wind: a wind blowing from behind a ship which helps it to move.

forecastle: a raised deck at the bow of a ship. Forecastles were built to protect the crew from attack.

freighter: a cargo ship. It is powered by an engine.

galley: a ship first built by the Greeks and Romans. Later, galleys were used as warships.

hold: the part of a ship where goods are carried.

horizon: the distant line where the sky and the sea or land appear to meet.

hovercraft: a type of ship which moves above the surface of the sea on a cushion of air. It is driven by propellers in the air.

hull: the main body or shell of a ship.

hydrofoil: a type of ship with foils which skim the surface of the water. It is driven by a propeller beneath the water.

inland waterway: a river or canal used by boats.

keel: the long piece of wood or metal which runs along the bottom of the hull and is the backbone of a ship.

lateen: a triangular sail.

liner: a ship carrying passengers that makes regular voyages at set times.

lock: a stretch of a canal with gates at each end. It is used to enable ships to go "uphill" or "downhill."

longship: a long, narrow ship built by the Phoenicians and the Vikings. It was used both for exploring and for fighting other ships.

maiden voyage: the first journey by a new ship.

mainmast: the tallest mast on a ship. It is usually in the middle of the ship.

nuclear power: the power produced by the heat made when atoms are split.

patrol: a regular voyage or flight. Patrol boats are often used to watch out for icebergs, changes in the weather or smugglers.

pike: a long pole with a pointed metal tip that was once used in battle.

pilot: a captain who takes charge of a ship entering or leaving harbor.

pitch: to plunge up and down in the sea. A ship pitches when the waves hit it at the bow of the ship.

Plimsoll line (mark): the line painted on the side of a ship. When the ship is fully loaded with cargo, the water level touches the line.

pollute: to spoil something. When oil is spilled from a ship, it pollutes the water and can kill fish and birds.

port: the left hand side of a ship.

propeller: a propeller is made of two or more twisted blades. As it turns, it pushes a ship forward.

propeller shaft: a shaft which connects the propeller to the ship's engine. As the shaft turns, the propeller spins.

radar: a way of finding the position of an object. Radio waves are sent out. When they meet an object, they bounce back to the radar set.

ram: a heavy piece of wood fastened to the bow of a warship and used to sink an enemy's ship.

reeds: dried stalks of plants found in marshy places.

roll: to sway from side to side. A ship rolls when the waves hit the side of the ship.

round ship: a cargo ship first used by the Phoenicians. Because the round ship was wider than a longship, it could take more cargo.

rudder: a hinged flat piece of wood or metal which is used to steer boats or planes.

sailcloth: a strong woven cloth used to make sails.

satellite: an object that people have launched into space. It sends back signals to earth.

starboard: the right hand side of a ship.

stern: the rear end of a ship.

sternwheeler: a type of paddle steamer with one paddle wheel at the stern.

tacking: sailing on a zig-zag course.

tanker: a ship built to carry liquids in bulk.

trimmed: moved from side to side to catch the wind.

turbine: a machine with many curved blades on a shaft. Steam makes the shaft turn around. The turning shaft drives a ship's propeller.

voyage: a long sea journey.

Index